MEMORIES
OF
STRATFORD ~ UPON ~ AVON

ALTON DOUGLAS
DENNIS MOORE
ADDITIONAL RESEARCH BY JO DOUGLAS

© 1993 ALTON and JO DOUGLAS.
ISBN 1 85858 010 2
Published by Brewin Books, Doric House, Church Street, Studley, Warwickshire B80 7LG.
Printed by Warwick Printing Co. Ltd., Theatre Street, Warwick CV34 4DR
Layout by Alton and Jo Douglas

Schofields, Wood Street, c. 1900.

Front cover:
Refreshment time with actor, Clive Morton, outside The Back Swan
(affectionately known as The Dirty Duck) c. 1965.

CONTENTS

...afy Warwickshire – leafier Stratford-upon-Avon. The ...wn lies at the heart of the heart of England, ideally ...aced on or near important lines of communication ...d has been described as a compact, mediaeval market-...wn with a minor Georgian town superimposed. Its ...me derives from the Old English, Straetford (a ford ... a Roman road) and Avon (British Celtic for 'river'). ...other source decides it is a ford where the important ...man road from Ryknild Street at Alcester reached ...atford. We have unearthed seven different spellings ...er than the present one and are, namely, Stretfordae, ...etforda, Stretford, Stratforde, Strafford, Stredford ...d Stretsed. There must be many more.

The Domesday Book (1086) records that 'the ...shop of Worcester holds 14^1/$_2$ hides [land units]; ...d for 31 ploughs; 21 villagers with a priest; 7 ...allholders have 28 ploughs; a mill, valued at 10 ...llings [50 pence]; 1,000 eels; a meadow 5 furlongs ... 2 furlongs.' The whole was valued before 1066 at ...0 shillings (£5) and in 1086 was priced at £25.

The growth and prosperity of most towns can be ...uged from the rise in population. At the end of the ...th century Stratford-upon-Avon had barely 3,000 ...k; 11,616 by 1931 with today's count being around ...,225.

The town had a railway of sorts by September 1826 ...en a 16 mile-long horse-tramway ran to Moreton-in-...arsh (Gloucs) and today has left its marks on the ...ges of the road from Stratford to Shipston-on-Stour. ...e brick bridge which carried this railway over the ...er now forms part of a leisure walk-way, passing close ... the Butterfly Farm and Jungle Safari. The main ...ad-bridge here, spanning the Avon, is Clopton ...idge, funds to build it having been provided by Sir ...gh Clopton around 1485. He became Lord Mayor ... London in 1492 and he also funded the rebuilding ... the Guild Chapel. This chapel marks the end of

Chapel Street and the start of Church Street. Next to the chapel is the Grammar School, originally the Guildhall of the Guild of the Holy Cross (1417), in which the Corporation met right up to the 19th century. The ground floor formed the Guildhall proper and the upper floor the Over Hall where William Shakespeare, Stratford's most famous son, would have studied as a pupil. This school has been a centre of learning since its founding in 1553. Today, 411 students are on its roll.

When approaching the town from the north, one senses a physical rise in temperature, so happily placed is this town in the general geographical setting. The residents' pride in the place is obvious. A National winner of the keenly-contested annual "Britain in Bloom" competition and a European finalist, the town has achieved considerable renown for the excellence of its floral displays. To walk through and about Stratford is a sheer delight. Boating and other riverside pleasures abound, whilst National Hunt racing at the Racecourse draws enthusiastic supporters. The World of Shakespeare, Waterside, offers a journey back in time to the authentic atmosphere of Elizabethan England. As exciting an experience as any is to join an official guided tour of The Memorial Theatre and its associated Swan Theatre (which was the original Memorial Theatre until its destruction by fire in 1926). This latter theatre, modelled on the concept of Shakespeare's 'Wooden O', is a masterpiece of faithful reconstruction.

Yet William Shakespeare, vital as he is to the town's success and prosperity, does not entirely overshadow the other activities, occasions, events and celebrations which the townspeople have been concerned with for so long. Join us in many of them in this book. Recall, reminisce and remember – here are Memories of Stratford-upon-Avon.

RATFORD-ON-AVON (10,427), Warwick. [*Map* 13.*D*.4.] London 90 miles.
1. 10–2, 6–10 w.d ; 12–2, 7–10 S.; 10–5, 6–10 M. Days. **M. Days**—Tues., Wed. Fri. **E. Closing**—Thurs. **Post**—7.30 p.m.
rking Facilities available.
arwick 8, Kenilworth 13, Stonebridge 21½, Lichfield 40½, Coventry 18½, Leamington
a 10½, Rugby 25, Daventry 27½, Northampton 39½◻ Barford 7½, Wellesbourne
astings 5½, Kineton 10, Banbury 20, Buckingham 37, Bicester 35, Long Compton
, Oxford 39½, Chipping Norton 21, Shipston-on-Stour 11, Moreton-in-Marsh 16½,
ckleton 9, Chipping Campden 11½, Broadway 15, Cheltenham 30◻ Evesham 14½,
wkesbury 28, Gloucester 38½, Ledbury 40◻ Alcester 8, Worcester 26, Leominster
, Droitwich 22, Tenbury Wells 44½, Ludlow 53½, Bromsgrove 20½, Kidderminster
, Bridgnorth 43½, Shrewsbury 64, Redditch 16◻ Henley-in-Arden 8, Birmingham
◻.

HOTELS.
** **Arden** (Unlic.) ; T.N.,46 ; 18 brms. ; S.R. 6/- to 9/- ; D.R. 12/- to 18/- ;
3/- ; L. 3/6 ; T. 1/6 ; H.T. to order ; D. 5/- ; Ch. from 8/6 ; R.W.T. ; G.A.—
. 4 ; 2/- N.
** **Red Horse**, Bridge Street ; T.N., 197 ; 80 brms. ; S.R. 7/6 to 8/6 ; D.R.
/- to 17/- ; B. 4/- ; L.c. 3/-· L.h. 4/- ; T. 1/6 ; D. 6/6 ; Ch. 10/- ; R.W.T. ;
.—L.u. 20 ; f.d.m. ; 2/- to 2/6 N.
** **Shakespeare**, Chapel Street ; T.N., 188 (Visitors), 60 (Management) ; 40
ns. ; S.R. 10/6 ; D.R. 15/6 to 17/6 ; B. 4/6 ; L.h. 5/- ; T. 2/- ; D. 7/- ; Ch.
/6 ; R.W.T. ; Pub. G. adj.
* **Falcon**, Chapel Street ; T.N., 187 ; 19 brms. ; S.R. 7/- to 7/6 ; D.R. 14/6
21/- ; B. 3/6 ; L.c. 3/- ; L.h. 3/6 ; T. 1/6 ; H.T. 3/6 ; D. 6/- ; Ch. 8/6 ; R.W.T. ;
.—C. 20 ; L.u. 2 ; f.d.m. ; 1/6 N.
* **White Swan**, Rother Street ; T.N., 157 ; 31 brms. ; S.R. & B. 9/- to
/6 ; D.R. & B. 18/- to 21/- ; L. 2/6 ; T. 1/6 ; D. 5/- ; Ch. 9/6 ; R.W.T. ; G.A.
. 10 ; L.u. 2 ; f.d.m. ; 2/- N. ; **T.H.**

GARAGES.
** A. **Bolland & Co.**, Guild and Henley Streets ; T.A., Bolland ; T.N., 14 ;
.—C. 80 ; M/C. 50 ; O.N. at call ; O.S. ; Ch. ; M/C. & R. ; B.E.
** F. **Guyver & Sons**, Henley and Rother Streets ; T.A., Guyver ; T.N.,
. G.A.—C. 100 ; M/C. 50 ; O.N. at call ; O.S. ; Ch.
** **Warwickshire County Garage**, Waterside ; T.N., 185 ; G.A.—C. 70 ;
N. at call ; O.S. ; Ch. ; M/C. & R. ; B.E.
1929

BEGINNINGS

Stratford-upon-Avon C. of E. School, 1913.

Infants' School, Broad Street, 1915.

Broad Street School, c. 1920.

Shottery School, c. 1925.

C. of E. School, Alcester Road, c. 1930.

Shakespeare's Birthday, New Place Gardens, 1936.

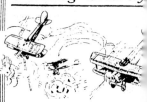

As a special Coronation treat, the Governors of the Memorial Theatre invite local children to see a performance of "A Midsummer Night's Dream", 1937.

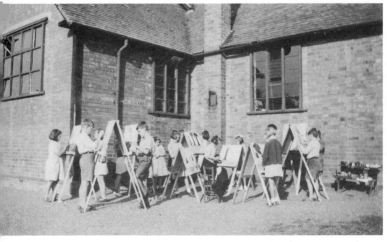

Art classes in the open, Shottery C. of E. Primary School, c. 1951.

St Gregory's R.C. Junior and Infants' School, St Gregory
Henley Street, Summer 1953.

Stratford-upon-Avon C. of E. Junior School, June 1959.

Two high
schools
go in on

STRATFORD boys
girls high schools will
next year to form a new
secondary school.

The plan has been ap
by the Secretary of Sta
Education, who gives Sep
1975 as the proposed da
the changeover. The ama
tion will bring sixth-for
velopment and the provis
appropriate additional faci

22.

8

Dress rehearsal, for a show at the Hippodrome, by Betty Lane's School of Dancing, 1963.

Pupils of King Edward VI School lead the procession to Shakespeare's tomb in the Parish Church, 23rd April 1967.

Youngsters from Lambert Special School prepare for a charity walk, sponsored by the Variety Club of Great Britain, 14th March 1979.

Officers and members of the 2nd Stratford-upon-Avon Boys' Brigade Company are joined, at their inauguration service, by members of the Girls' Brigade Company and their Chaplain, Rev. Frank Wiltshire, Payton Street Baptist Church, 1983.

The successful Stratford Grammar School for Girls' team, winners of the Warwickshire and Coventry Under 18 hocke tournament, October 1981.

Warwickshire Constabulary, Stratford-on-Avon Division, 1910.

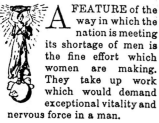

Recuperating soldiers, War Hospital, Clopton, 1917.

Bruce Bairnsfather, the well-known cartoonist, (left) with his father and brother at their home, Spa House, Bishopton, during the First World War.

Soldiers at the YMCA, Waterside, 1917.

War Hospital, Clopton, 1918.

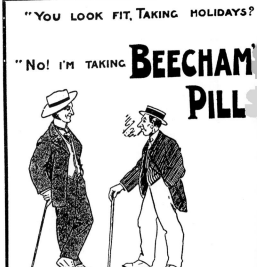
12

The Town Band, c. 1930.

Stratford Scouts' Bugle Band, c. 1930.

St John Ambulance Brigade, January 1931.

"Hitler Can Only Be Stopped by Force... I Know You Will All Play Your Part with Calmness and Courage"

PREMIER'S 11.15 A.M. CALL TO THE NATION

4.9.39

★ "I trust I may live to see the day when Hitlerism has been destroyed and a restored and liberated Europe has been re-established."

Leaving No. 10 with Mr. Chamberlain is a secretary carrying the Premier's gas mask and his own.

THE Prime Minister, broadcasting at 11.15 a.m. yesterday, said:—

I am speaking to you from the Cabinet Room at 10, Downing-street.

This morning the British Ambassador in Berlin handed the German Government a final Note stating that unless we heard from them by eleven o'clock that they were prepared at once to withdraw their troops from Poland a state of war would exist between us.

I HAVE TO TELL YOU NOW THAT NO SUCH UNDERTAKING HAS BEEN RECEIVED AND THAT CONSEQUENTLY THIS COUNTRY IS AT WAR WITH GERMANY.

You can imagine what a bitter blow it is to me that all my long struggle to win peace has failed.

Yet I cannot believe that there is anything more or anything different that I could have done and that would have been more successful.

Up to the very last it would have been quite possible to have arranged a peaceful and honourable settlement between Germany and Poland, but Hitler would not have it.

14   Control and Report Centre staff, ARP (Air Raid Precautions) c. 1940.

Home Guard members outside the Drill Hall, 1941.

Down Our Street

Bert is on the watch
for U boats
out on the Atlantic.
Under the same stars
Mum is on the watch
for fire bombs
down our street.
Dick is in Commandos
spraying with his
Tommy gun but
you should see father
on his stirrup pump.
Mr. Smith's a warden,
Jones is N.F.S.
Brown is an authority
on decontamination.
Robinson is ambulance,
marvellous with splints.
Mrs. R. is ready
with bandages and lints.
When the walls are falling
and the windows blaze
then you see some action
down our street.
Fire engines roaring —
quick the hoses out —
under debris crawling
to get the stricken out.
And where the fight is
thickest — look!
the canteen van . . .
Women cool as cucumbers
serving cups of tea!
Goering brought the
blitzkrieg to their firesides
but he couldn't break 'em:
now he never will.
Everybody's in it
down our street —
because everybody knows
that everybody's needed
— Down our street.

*   *   *   *

But Victory is not here yet. Therefore the word is : Still more service, still more saving. SAVE MORE.

. . . — Save for Victory

Home Guard Platoon parade near the Unicorn Hotel, now the Pen and Parchment, Bridge Foot, 1942.

"A" Flight, No. 1 Squadron, No. 9 I.T.W., June 1941. The squadron was billeted in Avonside and Avonfield Hotels.

15

Land Army girls, Stratford Nurseries, 1942.

Wings for Victory display, 1943.

Red Cross nurses and patients, Shottery Hall Auxiliary Hospital, Summer 1944

The ferry at Waterside
carries American soldiers,
on a local visit, 1944.

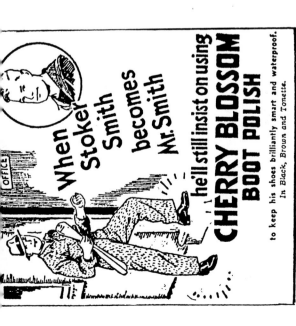
IN REMEMBRANCE OF THE HELP GIVEN BY THE
AMERICAN PEOPLE IN RAISING FUNDS FOR THE
BUILDING AND ENDOWMENT OF THE SHAKESPEARE
MEMORIAL THEATRE, AND TO COMMEMORATE
THE VISIT TO STRATFORD-UPON-AVON OF MANY
THOUSANDS OF OUR AMERICAN COMRADES IN
THE FIGHT FOR FREEDOM AND PEACE, THIS TABLET
IS GRATEFULLY DEDICATED BY THE GOVERNORS

The Staff of Stratford C. of E. Infant School, 1943.

STRATFORD	23.2.50
J PROFUMO (C)	21,492
R. Brown (Lab)	12,143
H. Seaborne (Lib)	4,318
Majority	9,349

A LARGE crowd gathered on the forecourt of the R. Shakespeare Theatre on Sunday afternoon, in presence of the Mayor and Mayoress, Councillor and David Bruce, and the chairman of Stratford Rural Cou. Mrs C S Harris, heard how the Ambulance Associa worried about the condition of their two ambulances, w had to be sent round the back streets because they m break down, had received two vehicles, one brand-n " out of the blue." 6.9.68

Warwickshire Constabulary, Stratford-on-Avon Division, September 1949.

EVENING T.W.G.

The March meeting of the Evening Townswomen's Guild, with a good company of members and visitors present, heard Mrs. Stafford, a quali-fied corsetière, give a most interesting and helpful talk, with three models bravely demonstrating the garments. A vote of thanks to them all was given by Mrs. I. Collett.

The drama and choir Chairmen re-ported much activity to provide the programme for a concert in April, while the handicraft group were busy with the exhibition arrangements. The social studies section is looking forward to a journey to Warwick. when interesting places will be visited with members of Warwick Guild.

The competition, won by the Chairman, for the best knitted article, was judged by Mrs. Stafford. The helpers, and especially Mrs. Sutton, who organised the recent rummage sale, were thanked for their work, over £21 being added to funds. A beetle drive, directed by Mrs. Rad-bourne, and refreshments served by the committee, ended the evening. 31.3.61

Town Clerk, Trevor Cox, seals the Centenary scroll, July 1969.

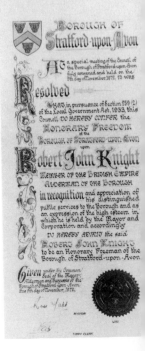

Putting the calendar back 100 years, the Town Council returns to the Upper Guildhall for the special meeting to open the Guild celebrations, 12th July 1969.

The Mayor, Councillor Malcolm Ray, and the Town Council, 1970.

Colonel Webb Owen, Commanding Officer of the Central Engineer Park at Long Marston, carries out the annual inspection of the King Edward VI School Combined Cadet Force, 15th May 1970.

Jan Roberts dresses the window of the Save the Children Shop, Sheep Street, 6th November 1973.

Some of the Stratford firemen who won the Warwickshire full-time fire brigade quiz, 31st January 1980. (From the left), Ray Hancox, Rod Abrahams, Roy Wathan and John Folland.

HOLY TRINITY CHURCH

STRATFORD-UPON-AVON

SERVICE OF DEDICATION

OF A MEMORIAL TO

9 INITIAL TRAINING WING

ROYAL AIR FORCE

1941 – 1944

Sunday, 16th June, 1991

at 1500 hours

Angus Maude, later Lord Maude of Stratford-upon-Avon, (right), acts as adviser to his son, Francis, who is compaigning to retain his marginal North Warwickshire Parliamentary seat, 19th May 1987.

Cyril Bennis and his wife, Roxanne, give the swans their Christmas morning treat, December 1989. Councillor Bennis is Stratford's voluntary swan-keeper and the couple are also well-known entertainers.

22

Celebrating the marriage of the Duke and Duchess of York, 1893.

RATFORD-ON-AVON CHRISTMAS STOCK SALE.

old-established event, which has long been
upon as an interesting institution of the
was held under the management of Messrs.
ngs and Deer at their sale-yard on Friday
e 14th inst. To those who can recal this
ng of the stalls and pastures fifteen or
years ago it need not be said that the present
on will not favourably compare with that
old time. Still the consignment of this
was a good and representative one, and
demonstrated the fact that the production of
beef and mutton is still well under-
and practised by the British farmer.
of the leading feeders of this well-
district were well represented on
ccasion, and the trade ruled brisk and
erative for the best quality.
t 120 animals of more or less grand quality
under the hammer, and amongst the lots
e named eight remarkably ripe shorthorn
f rare quality from the stalls of Mr. Wynn,
made an average of £26 15s 8d, the highest
being £30. Mr. H. Day, of Ailston, sent
ice and serviceable beasts—four neat heifers
w, and one ox—which were sold for an
o of £18 10s 10d, the top priced one
g £24. Mr. J. R. West was well represented
wonderfully compact and level Hereford
, which were readily disposed of at an aver-
£19 4s 2d, the highest price being £? ? ?s.
fers of Mr. Purser were a nice lot, and made
average. Mr. Cotterell Corbett was as usual
fore with four fine oxen of good Christmas
r. The average was £21 8s 9d. Mr.
yatt, whose reputation as a feeder is
known, sent ten animals of nice quality,
realised an average of £18 16s 5d, one of
t making £23. The four oxen of Mr. W.
rdan were of great scale, and with more
would have made grand specimens of the
orn beast. They made an average of
s 6d, the top price being £31. Mr. T. Mills
s usual, two heifers of considerable merit,
sold respectively for £20 5s and £21. Mr.
otter pitched three young cows of fine
y, which averaged £20 18s 4d. Mr.
Flower contributed two nice beasts, of
uality; and beasts of excellent quality, well
to the season, were sent by such well-known
ns Messrs. F. Crossley, Parker, Webb, R.
ow, M. C. Ashwin, J. Hawkes, R. Mansell,
Webb, M. Gibbons, S. Spencer, W. B.
s, Reading, Palmer, W. Wilson, Hews,
, Fairfax, and others. Three magnificent
lls, the property respectively of Mr.
Mr. Ashby, and Mr. R. Hawkes, were all of
quality, and made £31, £30 10s, and £27 5s
order named. 350 sheep were penned, many
d quality, and sold readily at good prices, and
le on the whole must be considered highly
ctory, well sustaining the character which
trict has always enjoyed.
1888

Mop Fair at the turn of the century.

Empire Day celebrations, Broad Street, c. 1905.

An explosion at the Gas Works, 1912.

Remembrance Day Parade, c. 1920.

Theatre Burned

1926, March 8: The Shakespeare Memorial Theatre at Stratford-upon-Avon perished in flames [on Saturday]. The quaintly picturesque building ensconced amid the trees on the bank of the Avon now lies a mass of ruins. The blackened sides of the roofless tower gape to the sky like the hideous mouth of some fabulous monster, the circular walls of the theatre itself, jagged and charred, enclose now a mere heap of debris with bricks and twisted ironwork protruding grotesquely from the black ashes of what was once the stage and the auditorium. Originating somewhere way back of the stage, the fire had secured a firm hold before it was discovered.

Floods in Waterside, 23rd May 1932.

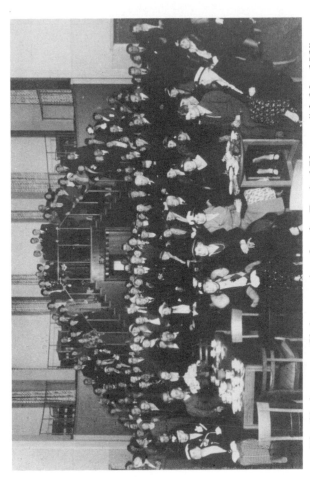

The Shakespeare Club reception for the Festival Players, 5th May 1935.

A crowded Bridge Street for the Birthday celebrations, 23rd April 1936. Note

Birthday Celebrations, April 1934.

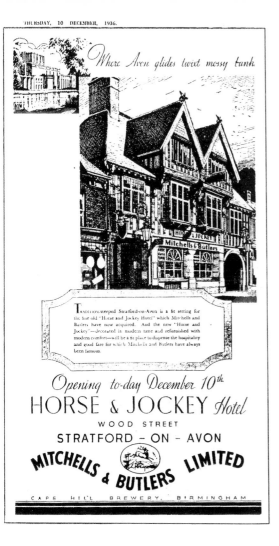

Nativity Play, Stratford C. of E. Infants' School, 1951.

The wedding of Philip Randall and Stella Clifford, St James Church, 1952. This was a typical scene, on so many occasions, at this fondly-remembered spot.

Coronation Party for the Nursery Class, Stratford C. of E. School, June 1953.

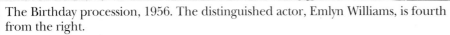

The Birthday procession, 1956. The distinguished actor, Emlyn Williams, is fourth from the right.

Broad Street School trip, c. 1956.

Film star, Greer Garson, visits An Hathaway's Cottage. c. 1955.

A toast to the re-opening of the sou section of the Stratford-on-Avon between Lapworth and Stratford, February 1964.

Broad Street School, c. 1958.

Mrs Hersey Flower (now Lady Flower) crowns the May Queen, Shottery C. of E. Primary School, c. 1962.

Lord Avon (former Prime Minister, Anthony Eden) in the tinted glasses, takes part, with his wife, in the Birthday parade, 1964

The Hon Eugene Black, chairman of the American Shakespeare Committee, opens the Shakespeare Centre, 23rd April 1964.

Christmas Party, Shottery C. of E. Primary School, c. 1965.

Mop Fair, 13th October 1964.

The demolition of the Church of St James, Guild Street, 14th June 1968.

Peter Wilson, Chairman of Sothebys, auctions items at the sale of exhibits from the Shakespeare Exhibition and Panorama, 4th October 1965.

Opening of the new TSB Bank premises, Meer Street, by Sir Athelstan Caröe, 31st May 1972. The Mayor, Councillor Ross Yates, was also manager of the Bank.

Fire destroys the Stratford Laundry Company, 23rd August 1965.

The Mayor and Mayoress at the opening of the re-furbished Boots' shop, Bridge Street, 1973.

Civic Sunday procession, 31st May 1970.

The Korean Ambassador and his family, with Dorothy Savage (steward) at the Shakespeare Birthday Celebrations, 1972.

Mr. Kenneth S. Kennedy
General Manager of the Stratford-upon-Avon Hilton
requests the pleasure of your company
at the Official Opening of the Hotel
on Wednesday, 14th March, 1973, at 11.45 for 12 noon
in the Grand Ballroom

RSVP
Stratford-upon-Avon Hilton   Buffet Lunche
Bridgefoot
Stratford-upon-Avon

Please bring this invitation with you

Celebrations follow the official opening of the Hilton (now The Moathouse), 14th March 1973.

The Mayor, Councillor Mrs Sarah Wheeler, releases balloons to mark the opening of the Bell Shopping Centre, 9th December 1976.

                                                    17 Grosvenor Place
                                                    SW1X 7HR

15th December 1972

Your Worshipful

On the occasion of the celebrations in Stratford-upon-
to mark Britain's entry into the European Communities,
it gives me special pleasure to convey, on behalf of
Ireland, greetings and best wishes to all the citizens
of your renowned township, the birthplace of William
Shakespeare, that genius whose influence is not only
European in character but also universal.

As of New Year's Day 1973, we are entered upon a new
voyage of discovery together and it is fitting that yo
citizens, who meet so many visitors from other countri
in Europe, should recognise this historic occasion in
manner worthy of your township's international fame.

Yours sincerely

Donal O'Sullivan
Ambassador

His Worshipful Mr Ross Yates
Mayor
Town Hall
Stratford-upon-Avon

Arms house opens with bang

CANNON fire echoed through the streets of Stratford on Thursday but it didn't worry the police.

For it wasn't the start of another civil war but the opening of a new arms and armour museum at Poet's Arbour in Sheep Street.

The Marquess of Hertford lit the cannon's touchpaper to salute its opening.

The museum is the brainchild of curator Robin Wigington. It will house a display of armour dating from the Middle Ages right up to the present day.

Among Mr Wigington's collection are suits of armour, pikes, swords, cannons, crossbows, axes, and a unique collection of pistols and guns made specially for Tipu Sultan, the Tiger of Mysore.

The museum is open to the public. 9.4.82

A bar at the White Swan Hotel is named after the town's other literary genius. Philip Baughan (right) suggested the name and hotel manager, Frank Stubbs, helps him to mark the event, 24th November 1982.

Gyles Brandreth, broadcaster and now an M.P., opens the world's biggest Teddy Bear museum, Greenhill Street, 30th June 1988.

Vehicles and drivers assemble at Charlecote Park, for the lunch break, during the Shakespeare Run, 7th September 1987.

35

Stratford Carnival, 15th July 1989.

Join the Bard's celebrations

Its historical, full of pageantry, ablaze with colour — and a sightseer's dream!

Its William Shakespeare's birthday, being celebrated in Stratford-upon-Avon on April 23rd — Midline Day.

This is a day when Stratford comes alive with the flags of every nation and lays on a spectacle which has become famous the world over.

Ceremony

Artists, musicians, dignitaries and ambassadors honour the Bard of Avon in a ceremony which begins in the morning and lasts until long after the night is out . . .

Guide Friday open-top buses will meet you at the station from the 1109, 1209, 1309 and 1409 arrivals, and can take you on a guided tour of the Shakespeare properties. Or if you prefer to "do your own thing", just stroll at your leisure through this delightful country town with its fine central river and canalside areas, its open spaces, parks and places to sit. Take in a drink or a meal in one of the many old pubs, restaurants and cafes dotted around this ancient town.

And why not wander around the quaint streets and alley-ways and browse to your heart's content in the multitude of shops where the new has tastefully blended in with the old to retain all the original charm and character. Purchase the usual commodities, buy yourself a souvenir or search for that "old master" among the many antique shops!

Extravaganza

Your visit to Stratford-upon-Avon would not be complete without a call at the "World of Shakespeare" on Waterside, a million pound extravaganza that recreates the sights and sounds of a bygone era. With a Day Ranger or Supertripper ticket, adults get 50p off the admission price.

Stratford is just one of the many places available to you on Midline Day. Make the best use of your Day Ranger ticket. *1988*

"Miss World" competitors add even more beauty to Anne Hathaway's Cottage, 1981.

● Pedal post. . .The new and the old came together during Tuesday's downpour when the Post Office took delivery of its redesigned bicycle, built by Stratford cycle manufacturers W R Pashley Ltd, which will be distributed to postmen and women all over the country.

Stratford postie Steven Nokes, right, puts the new cycle through its paces alongside a replica of its 1880 predecessor with the appropriately dressed Keith Maddox at the handlebars.

It is the first time the Royal Mail bikes have been re-designed in 60 years. The new model has three-speed gears, all-weather hub brakes, mountain bike style handlebars and virtually indestructible plastic mudguards. *22.9.92*

ROYAL VISITS

1932, April The Prince of Wales on Saturday opened the Shakespeare Memorial Theatre at Stratford-upon-Avon in the presence of the Governors, ambassadors of several countries and other distinguished guests. A procession passed to the Poet's tomb in Holy Trinity Church where wreaths were laid.

[The theatre opened with a large stock of costumes and scenery, gifts from supporters: and the balance of the funds raised, £100,000, was invested to ensure annual income. By 1935 accommodation had proved inadequate and the dress circle and the balcony were extended forward without affecting the architectural character of the interior.]

Mary, the Princess Royal (centre), enters the Red Cross Hospital, Shottery Hall, followed by Lady Helen Seymour, 6th July 1944

Red Letter Day

1950, April 21: The first visit by a reigning monarch to Stratford-upon-Avon was that yesterday of King George VI, accompanied by the Queen and Princess Margaret. They attended a performance of *Henry VIII* at the Memorial Theatre.

The Vicar of Stratford-upon-Avon, Canon Noel Prentice, takes the King and Queen and Princess Margaret into Holy Trinity Church, 20th April 1950.

The Queen and The Duke of Edinburgh visit the Memorial Theatre for a performance of "As You Like It", 15th June 1957.

The Duke of Edinburgh tours the Shakespeare Exhibition, 24th April 1964.

Princess Margaret and her husband, Lord Snowdon, are greeted by House Manager, Sean McCarthy, prior to the performance of "Coriolanus", 1st August 1967.

The Queen Mother visits the town, 1st June 1974.

The Queen, accompanied by Mr C.M.T. Smith-Ryland, Lord Lieutenant of Warwickshire, walks through the town during her visit to mark the Royal Shakespeare Theatre's centenary, June 1975.

...ncess Alexandra unveils the plaque to commemorate her opening the Police Station, Rother Street, 30th November 1978.

THIS THEATRE WAS OPENED BY
Her Royal Highness
The PRINCESS ANNE
ON TUESDAY, MAY 29th 1979

AN ELIZABETHAN PAGEANT
THE HERITAGE THEATRE
STRATFORD·UPON·AVON

The Prince of Wales on a visit to the Swan Theatre, 22nd April 1991.

The Duke of Kent and Trust Director, Dr Levi Fox, admire the may tree beside Shakespeare's Birthplace,
7th May 1988. The Duke was in town to take part in a tree-planting ceremony at Anne Hathaway's
Cottage and to open the latest attraction, a garden of trees and shrubs.

AT WORK

Staff of Trinity College, c. 1880.

John Harris & Sons at work, Rowley Crescent, c. 1890.

Foster Clark's
The Creamiest and most economical Custard obtainable, delicious flavour, absolutely pure, and most nourishing. **The Cream of All Custards.**
Cream Custard

JOHN HARRIS & SONS
of Stratford Ltd
EST. 1875

Building Cemetery Lodge, Evesham Road, 1881. John Harris, founder of John Harris & Sons and grandfather of the present owners, stands (plans in hand) on the scaffolding.

White's, saddlers, 13 Bridge
Street, c. 1890.

R.M. Bird & Co., Wine Merchants, Bridge Street, c. 1895.

Wood Street, c. 1895.

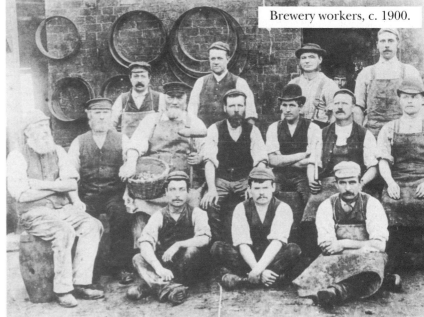

Brewery workers, c. 1900.

Fincher & Co., Ely Street, c. 1900.

Henley Street, c. 1903. This is the site of the present library.

Wood Street, c. 1910.

36 High Street, c. 1905.

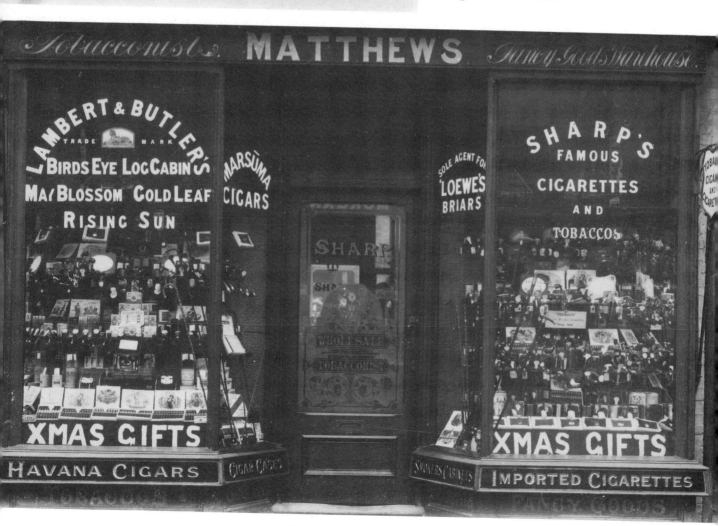

High Street, 1910.

The Cattle Market, 1906.

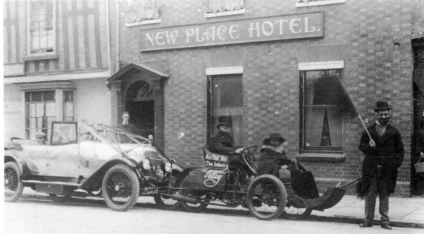

Launching a new Riley, with a look back to earlier times, next to New Place Gardens, c. 1924.

11 Sheep Street, c. 1911.

16, Greenhill Street, c. 1925.

Waiting for the rush, c. 1925.

Stratford Midland Junction, c. 1925.

Brand-new and ready to go, Waterside, 1st January 1932.

49

The first day of trading in their new premises, T.C. H[...]
butchers, Bull Street, 1934.

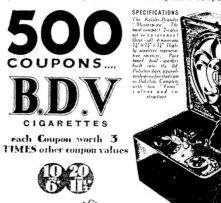

The staff of Lennard's Shoe Shop, with their [...]
window display presentation, 36 High Street, c. [...]

Hutchings & Co., New Broad Street, c. 1940.

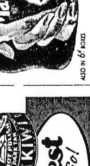

Beckett's, 43 Wood Street, c. 1953.

Peter Slevin, Warwickshire's youngest master thatcher, works on the re-thatching of Ann Hathaway's Cottage, Shottery, 26th March 1954.

Bottling Plant workers, Flowers' Brewery, Brewery Street, 1960.

Harry Davies repairs barrels, Flowers' Brewery, 26th June 1967.

Windsor Street, 14th April 1977.

54

Re-roofing the Shakespeare Birthplace Trust premises, Henley Street, 1988.

Pedestrianisation is underway, Henley Street, Spring 1989.

E NEWSPAPER YOU CHOOSE TO READ

Stratford · UPON · AVON · Herald

'I wish no other Herald, no other speaker of my living actions' — Shakespeare

Scouts F.C., 1912/13.

Stanley Matthews, hotly pursued by Town Clerk, Trevor Cox (now District Secretary and Solicitor) puts in the pass that leads to the Entertainers' first goal.

Stratford-upon-Avon Herald, 20th October, 1972

First knight of soccer at Stratford

A BONUS for the 700 or so spectators at Sunday's fund-raiser between Midland Press and The Entertainers was the appearance of Sir Stanley Mathews, who had phoned one of the organisers the previous day to ask: "Do you think they'd let me play?"

Play he did, throughout the 90 minutes, alongside the other Stanley Matthews, his tennis-playing son.

But before comedian Dave King and his Entertainers XI took the field there was a women's soccer match — also, surprisingly, of 90 minutes and played with intense rivalry—be-tween Aston Villa and Coventry Bantams. Few had mastered any of the soccer skills though they knew the routines. In fact it was too routine at times to be excit-ing. It was important to them and their supporters, however.

They all enjoyed it, especially Bantams, who won in a close finish by 4-3.

Then Sea Cadets of TS "Gurkha" gave a demonstration

in which they raised a mast, test of their seamanship in whi they lashed together a pair oars, hoisted them and the fla and were inspected by the Em of Wootton Wawen and his u likely looking entourage.

After these appetisers can the main course, in which Mi land Press, with Aston Villa Ron Wylie adding bite, threa ened at first to make a meal the Entertainers, leading deser edly 2-0 at half-time.

The first goal was a crack from Pat Foley, the type whi Stratford Town regulars ha seen from him before though too infrequently. The second w an own goal.

After the interval Stratford town clerk Trevor Cox came c as substitute to add some loc flavour, Dave King hit a po with a "generous" penalt netted the rebound but was n allowed to get away with that referee Ernie Hunt and the sco remained at 2-0 until some real good play by big centre-forwar Jeremy Bulloch and Craig Dou las eventually had its effect.

For the first goal the chunk fast-moving Roy Holder was p in possession by Sir Stanley-who elected to play a midfie role rather than perform his cu tomary touchline tricks — b Holder still had a lot to do ar it was a very good shot that h hammered past keeper Joh McShane.

Only seven minutes from tin Roy Holder again scored we with an equalising shot just i side McShane's left post.

Second Stratford Boys' Brigade, Junior Section Company, with the Coventry and District Boys' Battalion KO Cup. (Back) James Salmon, Ben McKendry, Mark McLoughlin (goal scorer), Kai Coombes, Jamie Compton (goal scorer), Simon Blore and Daniel Hatcher. (Front) Martin Proctor, Carlo Giorgio (goal scorer), Colin Ireland, captain Iain Herdman (four goals), Allan Murphy (five goals) and Paul Bell. They beat the Tenth Coventry Company in the final, 12-0. (Photo: Morris Troughton.) *1985*

Stratford Alliance F.C., 11th November 1989.

Actors' cricket team, c. 1960.

Stratford Cricket Club, 22nd June 1991.

gory's R.C. Junior and Infants' School Netball Team, 1972.

Stratford-upon-Avon Falcons, 1977. The basketball team were sponsored by American Dream Ice Cream.

The Bowling Club, c. 1969.

Stratford R.F.C., 11th November 1989.

Police Tug-o-War Team, 1947.

Golf at The Welcombe Hotel, 23rd July 1983.

The start of the Boy Scouts' Marathon Race, c. 1915.

Hippodrome Roller Skating Rink, Boxing Day, 1939.

9.4.13

IE Cyclecar Club's rally at Stratford-on-Avon,
with stopping and restarting tests on Sunrising
Hill, were held last week-end, and proved an
enormous success. Hundreds of Midland
ists and motorcyclists were present at these
vents, and by their presence gave the cycle-
s who had come up from London a splendid wel-
some 500 gathering at Stratford.
meet on Saturday was at the end of the Edg-
Road tramway, and by 2.30 p.m. the following
started:—Mr. A. C. Armstrong (G.N.), Mr.
child (Globe), Mr. W. G. McMinnies (Morgan
car "The Jabberwock"), Mr. A. P. Bradley
, Mr. Phillips (Warne), Mr. Cleave (Sabella),
Nash (G.N.) and Mr. Kreitmeyer (Zebra).
l motorcyclists accompanied the party, and
cyclecars joined in en route, Mr. de Peyrecave
meeting the party at Banbury.

key Team, Clopton School, 1922/23.

Chris Ward, from Stratford-upon-Avon (2nd left), a member of
the Warwickshire fencing team that won the Inter-County
Tournament at Henley College, 16th September 1980.

61

Broad Street School group, the Bathing Place, Warwick Road, c. 1930.

The Boat Club row on the Avon, 19th May 1981.

Possibly the most famous car in the world, Chitty Chitty Bang Bang, is owned by Pierre Picton (who describes himself as an "eccentric local character") and is housed not far from Anne Hathaway's Cottage.

THE DIRTY DUCK
STRATFORD UPON AVON

63

"Chorus Line of '46", High School.

Saturday Night Dance

THE HIPPODROME,

SATURDAY, 7th MAY, 1955

FRED NEWEY AND HIS QUINTET

Dancing 8—11.45 p.m.   Admission 3/6   Buffet

7.15 p.m. Advanced Class, 8 p.m. Mrs. De-Bastion will give a talk and demonstration, "The Dress to Wear for Dancing"; 9 p.m. General Dancing.

Ballet class, The Memorial Theatre, in the mid-19

Shakespeare Morris Men, one of the town's most colourful attractions, 24th April 1976.

Stratford-upon-Avon Chamber Music Society

Jump 'n Jivers, King Pleasure and the Biscuit Boys, appear at the Festival, 15th July 1991.

The World of Shakespeare

WATERSIDE, STRATFORD-UPON-AVON

1929, June 7: In a report by the Governors of the Shakespeare Memorial Theatre, issued yesterday, it was stated that to build a theatre on the lines suggested by the architects and director, after a tour of Continental centres to inspect theatres, would cost £250.000.

[The plan ultimately adopted was for an auditorium for 1,000, a stage 121ft. wide in front, 55ft. at rear and 45ft. deep, ample foyer and refreshment rooms leading to a river terrace, with attention to adequate and comfortable dressing-rooms, at an inclusive cost of £150.000: but the foundations, owing to vicinity of the river, gave extra trouble, and added £23.913 to the cost. Work began on January 31, 1929, the foundation stone was laid by Lord Ampthill on April 2, 1929, and the work was completed by January 31 1932.]

This time, Iago proves to be the steadying influence as Emlyn Williams restrains Harry Andrews, as Othello, 30th May 1956.

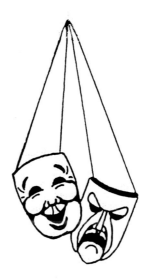

SHAKESPEAR
Memorial Theat
STRATFORD-UPON-AV
Director: SIR BARRY JACKS
Gen. Manager: LEONARD CRAIN

1947 FESTIV

APRIL 5th TO SEPTEMBE

ROMEO AND JULIET
DOCTOR FAUSTUS (Marlowe)
MEASURE FOR MEASURE
LOVE'S LABOUR'S LOST
TWELFTH NIGHT
THE TEMPEST
RICHARD II
THE MERCHANT OF VENICE
PERICLES
PRINCE OF TYRE

Beatrix Lehmann   Robert Harris
Walter Hudd   Paul Scofield
John Ruddock   Veronica Turle
Dudley Jones   Michael Golden
Laurence Payne   Daphne Slater

Evenings 7.30.   Matinees Wednes
Saturdays and Easter Monday, 2.
Reserved Seats ——— 4/- to 10/-
BOX OFFICE OPEN 10.30 a.m.
6 p.m. (Stratford-upon-Avon 227)
Please send stamped envelope fo
circular.

Shakespeare Memorial Theatre
Directed by GLEN BYAM SHAW CBE
General Manager and Licensee GEORGE HUME

AS YOU LIKE IT
BY WILLIAM SHAKESPEARE

.. ..	RICHARD JOHNSON
.. ..	JAMES WELLMAN
.. ..	DEREK MAYHEW
.. ..	ROBIN LLOYD
the Wrestler	RON HADDRICK
.. ..	JANE WENHAM
.. ..	PEGGY ASHCROFT
ONE	PATRICK WYMARK
.. ..	PETER CELLIER
EDERICK	MARK DIGNAM
SHED DUKE	CYRIL LUCKHAM
.. ..	REX ROBINSON
RD	ANTONY BROWN
ORD	PETER PALMER
GE	PETER WHITMARSH
AGE	MICHAEL SAUNDERS
.. ..	DONALD ECCLES
.. ..	ROBERT ARNOLD
.. ..	ROBERT HARRIS
.. ..	STEPHANIE BIDMEAD
R MARTEXT	DONALD LAYNE-SMITH
.. ..	DOREEN ARIS
.. ..	TOBY ROBERTSON
.. ..	GORDON WRIGHT
E BOYS	JOHN MURRAY SCOTT

s, Attendants and Foresters :
y TAPPER, MAVIS EDWARDS, ELIZABETH EVANS, PAMELA TAYLOR, THANE
NY, BARRY WARREN, EDWARD CADDICK, SIMON CARTER, JOHN DAVIDSON,
DAVIES, WILLIAM ELMHIRST, KENNETH GILBERT, JULIAN GLOVER, JOHN
SON, NORMAN MILLER, JOHN SALWAY, GORDON SOUTER, ROY SPENCER,
TOPHER BOND.

2.4.57.

Paul Robeson (Othello) gets to grips with Sam Wanamaker (Iago), 7th April 1959.

l Luckham (Quince), on the left, Ian Holm
ck) and Charles Laughton (Bottom), below,
earse the play within a play, "A Midsummer
Night's Dream", 3rd June 1959.

Tony Church (Hortensio), Elizabeth Sellars (Bianca) and
Peter Jeffrey (Lucentio) rehearse a scene from
"The Taming of the Shrew", 22nd June 1960.

67

John Slater.

Best wishes to you
Sincerely
Laurence Harvey

Laurence Harvey.

All good wishes
Dorothy Tutin.

Dorothy Tutin.

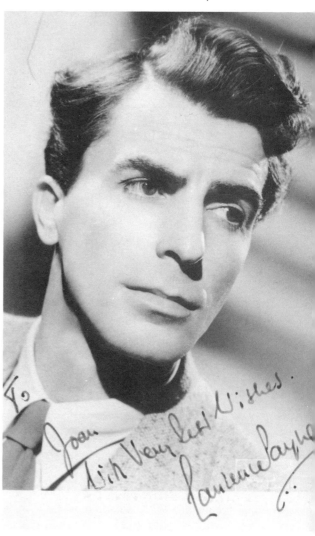

To
Joan
with very best wishes.
Laurence Payne

Laurence Payne.

Michael Hordern.

Claire Bloom.

John Nettles, star of the TV series "Bergerac" and one of the most recent additions
to the ranks of the Royal Shakespeare Company.

Michael Redgrave (centre) performs in "Garrick's Ode", Town Hall, 23rd June 1957.

Peter Pears (left) and Richard Pascoe (right) rehearse with Princess Grace of Monaco
for the Poetry Festival, 10th July 1977.

B.B.C.'s New Offer to Dance Band Leaders

1936

By Our RADIO CORRESPONDENT.

LONDON, Thursday.

OFFICIALS of the B.B.C. were to-day engaged in preparing new terms to be offered to radio dance bands following upon the conference at Broadcasting House yesterday.

Although all present were sworn to secrecy I gather that the B.B.C. made clear that they would refuse to negotiate further unless the dance band leaders were prepared to withdraw the ban on the signing of new contracts. If the dance band leaders are agreeable to doing this the B.B.C. on their part would make any agreement reached retrospective, dating from 4 January.

Amicable Terms

This was the extent of the business transacted, but the representatives of the B.B.C. intimated that they would draw up a new offer and submit it to the dance band leaders within the next day or two.

The B.B.C. offer rejected by the dance band leaders was one of £3 per man plus a fee for orchestrations, whereas the Dance Band Directors' Association asked for £5 per man, plus orchestration fees.

Opinion among dance band leaders is that amicable terms will be arranged and that there will be no interruption of dance music programmes. Harry Roy and Bert Ambrose, however, are expected to continue to refuse to broadcast.

Vera Lynn.

Bebe Daniels and Ben Lyon.

Harry Roy.

Richard Hearne.

Gracie Fields.

Bernard Braden

Semprini.

Sunday's TV programmes

BBC	LONDON	NORTH & MIDLANDS
2.30 p.m. Gardening.	11.15 a.m. Service from the Free Church, Hampstead Garden Suburb.	11.15 a.m. Service.
3.0 News Review.		2.30 p.m. ABC Investigates with Simon Kester.
3.30 Concert Hour—BBC Symphony Orchestra.	2.15 p.m. Armand and Michaela Denis in Africa.	3.0 Richard Hearne in "The Butler's Dilemma" (film).
4.15 Brains Trust.	2.30 Free Speech.	4.35 Bid for Fame.
5.0 Children.	3.0 Liberace	5.15 Children.
6.12 Weather.	3.30 "This England" (film) with John Clements and Constance Cummings.	6.5 News.
7.0 Religious talk—on Christmas.		6.45 Christmas Books.
7.25 News.	4.50 Children	7.25 News.
7.30 On Stage — Excerpts from "Share My Lettuce" at the Comedy Theatre, London.	6.5 News.	7.30 William Gargan and Brian Reece in "Racing Car."
	6.45 About Religion	8.0 Sunday Night at the Prince of Wales, with Gracie Fields.
8.0 Yvonne Mitchell and Freda Jackson in "The Trial of Marie Lafarge" (play).	7.25 News.	9.0 Ron Randell in "Operation Yo-Yo."
	7.30 I Love Lucy.	
	8.0 Sunday Night at the Prince of Wales —with Gracie Fields.	
9.30 Zoo Quest — Pigmies and Paradise Birds.	9.0 Highway Patrol.	9.30 "The Dividing Line" (play).
	9.30 "The Dividing Line" (play).	
10.0 Max Jaffa's Trio.	10.30 News.	10.30 News.
10.30 News.	10.35 The Jack Jackson Show.	10.35 Jack Jackson Show.
10.50 Epilogue.	11.5 Box Office.	11.5 Box Office.
	11.30 Epilogue	11.30 Epilogue.

SCOTLAND 2.15 p.m. Armand and Michaela Denis in Africa. 2.30 Free Speech. 3.0 The Rosemary Clooney Show. 3.30 "The Mill on the Floss" (film). 4.50 Children. 6.5 News. 6.45 About Religion. 7.25 News. 7.30 I Love Lucy. 8.0 Sunday Night at the Prince of Wales. 9.0 Highway Patrol. 9.30 "The Dividing Line" (play). 10.30 News. 10.35 Jack Jackson Show. 11.5 "The Stolen Pearl" (play).

15.12.57

Wilfred Pickles

Sunday's Radio

LIGHT	HOME
8.0 a.m. Silver Chords.	7.50 a.m. Sunday reading.
9.30 "Hutch."	8.0 News.
9.45 The Archers.	8.15 BBC Concert Orchestra.
10.30 Top of the Form.	9.0 News.
11.0 Have a Go!	9.10 Home for the Day.
11.30 Congregational service from Purley, Surrey.	9.45 Service.
12.0 Family Favourites.	10.30 Music Magazine.
1.15 p.m. Billy Cotton Band Show.	11.20 Records.
1.45 Educating Archie.	12.10 p.m. The Critics.
2.15 Ray's a Laugh.	1.0 News.
2.45 Movie-Go-Round.	1.10 Coast and Country — Hay-on-Wye.
3.30 Melody Hour.	1.40 Opera records.
4.30 "Beau Geste" (part 3).	2.0 Gardening.
5.0 Mr. Bentley and Mr. Braden.	2.30 Symphony concert.
5.30 The Hit Parade.	3.15 Flying—historical talk.
6.0 Popular songs, old and new.	3.30 Symphony concert (contd.).
6.30 Round the Bend.	4.15 The Rent Act.
7.0 Semprini.	4.30 Talking About Music.
7.30 News.	5.0 Children.
7.35 Request records.	6.0 News.
8.30 Hymns from the Wesley Memorial Church, Epworth, Lincs.	6.15 Radio Newsreel.
	6.45 Grand Hotel.
9.0 Confidentially—They're Off!	7.30 Letter from America.
9.30 Does the Team Think?	7.45 Service.
10.0 Ian Stewart (piano).	8.25 Appeal.
10.30 News.	8.30 "Soames Forsyte, Esq."
10.40 Pick of the Pops.	9.0 News.
11.30 Felix King (piano).	9.15 Anglo-American Relations —lecture.
11.50 The End of the Day.	9.45 Helen Watts (contralto), London Harpsichord Ensemble.
11.55 News.	10.30 Short story.
	10.50 The Epilogue.
	11.0 News.

LUXEMBOURG 5.0 p.m. Beaver Club. 6.15 You Lucky People. 6.45 Accordion Time. 7.0 David Whitfield Show. 7.30 Winifred Atwell Show. 8.0 Opportunity Knocks, with Hughie Green. 8.30 Take Your Pick. 9.0 This I Believe. 9.30 All the Vaughans—music and song. 10.0 Record Rendezvous. 10.30 Bing Sings 10.45 Ted Heath and his music. 11.0 Top Twenty.

Billy Cotton.

Winifred Atwell.

Tony Hancock, one of the popular radio & TV come of the fifties and sixties.

The Maydels.

One of our busiest actors, Don Henderson, has lived in the town for over twenty six years. His wife, Shirley Stelfox, is frequently seen in television plays and sit-coms. Coincidentally, Alton appeared in his first radio play with Don in 1987.

Actress, Hedli Niklaus and her husband, actor, Leon Tanner, pictured at their Stratford home. Apart from their other achievements, Hedli is a regular in the long-running "Archers" radio serial (as Kathy Perks) and Leon is currently appearing at the Haymarket Theatre in London in "Cyrano de Bergerac", 1992.

A proposed new cinema for Bridge Foot, which did not materialise, 1937.

Projection Room, Picture House, Greenhill Street, c. 1933.

Norman Painting, host of the documentary "Shakespeare in Trust", 1984. Since its inception, in 1950, he has appeared as Phil Archer in the BBC radio serial "The Archers".

Dean Martin Jerry Lewis, appearing at Picture House this week.

Shakespeare's birthplace, Henley Street, c. 1850.

The original Memorial Theatre, c. 1905.

Red Horse Hotel, Bridge Street, c. 1905.
This is now occupied by Marks & Spencer.

21/12/1888

DOWNING AND PARKHOUSE,

MARKET CROSS, STRATFORD-ON-AVON.

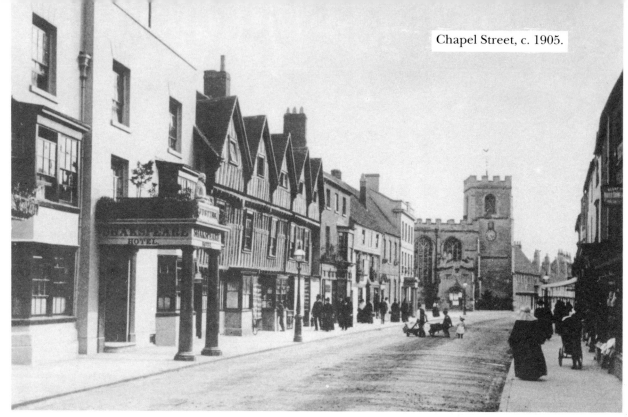

Chapel Street, c. 1905.

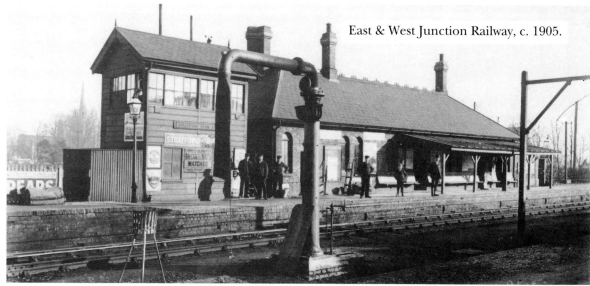

East & West Junction Railway, c. 1905.

GWR station, Alcester Road, c. 1910.

Lucy's Lock, c. 1910.

HENLEY STREET, STRATFORD-ON-AVON.

STRATFORD-ON-AVON.

At Stratford, the stranger should make a point of seeing the following, if nothing else:—

Shakespeare's Birthplace and Museum (Henley Street, open week-days 9 a m. to 6 p.m. in summer, 9 to dusk in winter. Admission 1/-).

Holy Trinity Church (admission 6d.), containing tomb and bust of poet.

Shakespeare Memorial Theatre and Library, open 10 a.m. to 6 p.m. in summer, 4 p.m. winter. Admission 6d.

The Group Group of Statuary close by.

SHAKESPEARE'S HOUSE,
STRATFORD-ON-AVON.

STRATFORD-ON-AVON.—*Continued.*

The New Place Gardens, open from 10 a.m. to dusk during the summer.

The New Place Museum, open from 9 to 6 (admission 6d.).

The Guild Chapel nearly facing the New Place Gardens, with, on its south side **the Guild Hall and Grammar School.** Nearly opposite the latter is the residence of Miss Marie Corelli. **Anne Hathaway's Cottage,** about 1 mile from Stratford, open from 9 a.m. to dusk in winter; summer 9 to 6. Admission 6d.

78

High Street, c. 1910.

Chapel Street, 1912.

High Street, c. 1920.

Ox-roasting during the Mop, c. 1929.

Rother Street, c. 1929.

Shottery Church Choir, c. 1935.

COUNCIL NOT PREPARED TO PAY ROAD BILL

BUILDERS TO BEAR COST THEMSELVES

£1,400 SERVICE SCHEME
1936

A PLAN for the development of 85 acres of land as a garden city has been rejected by Stratford-on-Avon Council because a majority of the members objected to bearing the cost of five new roads on the estate.

The proposal of the Council's Town-planning and Plans Committee was that approval be given to the lay-out of the estate which fronts on Knight's-lane and Loxley-road and that the Council should undertake to make the five service roads and lay greenswards at a cost of £1,400.

The Council were told that Mr. H. J. Brueton, of Birmingham—who is developing the estate—was prepared to give, free of all charge to the Council, the land required for roads and greens.

Sir Archibald Flower, committee chairman, stated that it was at first proposed to build straight rows of houses—in which Mr. Brueton would merely have been following the bad example already set in housing by the Council itself—but Mr. Brueton had met the committee in a friendly spirit, and the estate would now be developed "on garden city lines."

For that the Council should be grateful to Mr. Brueton.

Make out your shopping list from this...

9.11.39

EGGS are up again. They are now: (a) home produced fresh, large 3s., medium 2s. 6d., small 2s. a doz.; (b) Eire fresh, large 2s. 6d., small 2s. 3d. a doz.; (c) European fresh, large 2s. 3d., small 2s. a doz.; (d) others, large 1s. 9d., small 1s. 6d. a doz.

Butter: 1s. 7d. a lb.
Imported lard: 6d. a lb.
Condensed milk: Full cream sweetened, large 8½d., small 4¾d.; full cream unsweetened, large 6½d., small 3½d.; skimmed, large 5½d.
Potatoes: Grade A. 1¼d. a lb., or 8d. for 7lbs.; Grade B. 1d. a lb., or 7d. for 7lbs.
Dried fruits: Dates, unstoned 4½d., stoned 5½d.; figs. 6½d.; currants, 7d.; sultanas, 8d.; raisins, 8d., or if stoned in the United Kingdom, 9½d.; plums and prunes, 8½d.; apples, pears, peaches, nectarines, fruit salad, 10d.; apricots, 1s. 3d.; muscatels (in cartons), 2s. a lb. Dried fruits sold in packets may be sold for 1d. to 6½d. more.
Sugar: Granulated, 4½d.; cubes, 5d.; castor, 5d.;

pieces, 4½d.; soft brown, 4½d.; Demerara, 4¾d.; preserving, 4¾d.; icing, 5½d.; Barbados, 5½d.
Fish: Fresh herrings, 6d. a lb.; bloaters, 8d. a lb.; kippers, 10d. a lb.
Canned salmon, in three grades, the most expensive being 1s. 7½d. (flats), 1s. 4d. (talls).
(All these are maximum prices.)

★

Shops selling canned salmon, eggs, sugar, imported lard and butter must put up a list of maximum prices of these in a conspicuous position.

Butcher's meat, margarine, cooking fats, and tea must not be sold for more than their prices at the end of August, according to the Food Orders: but margarine is now of standard quality at 6d. a lb., and we have had a number of letters saying that butchers have increased prices. If you know any clear case of this you should complain to your local food controller.

YOU WILL FIND UP-TO-THE-MINUTE FOOD PRICES ON THIS PAGE EACH THURSDAY.

EGGS 3/- doz

SMALL EGGS 2/- doz

BUTTER 1/7 lb

8½d

PRUNES 8½ lb

1¼d lb

6d lb

CARS ARE SHOWING TOO MUCH LIGHT 1940

Motorists should overhaul their lamps. Police are keeping a special watch on car lights.

Observations from the air show that many motorists are not complying with the regulations. Many side lights are much too bright and headlamp masks are defective or wrongly adjusted.

Dazzling is sometimes caused by the lamp getting tilted, or by the mask twisting round.

Only one headlamp may be used, except in fog. Buses and coaches can carry two headlamps

White paint on the backs of cars is getting dingy in many cases, and drivers should see that it is kept fresh and clean.

A pamphlet on how to dim car lights can be had at police stations.

BE SURE YOU HAVE A GAS MASK

If you have no gas mask discover at once the name and address of your Air Raid Warden and go to him. You can obtain the information from your Town Hall.

And if you are going away for any length of time remember to take your gas masks with you. Those who ignore this advice may be running grave risks.

Thirdly, make thorough preparations to obscure all lighting.

Staffs in London stores were doubled yesterday to cope with the rush to buy black-out materials.

25.8.39.

RUBBER SHORTAGE

EVERY DRIVER MUST HELP NOW!

Lorry drivers, taxi-drivers, private motoris you can do more than anybody (1) To he conserve the nation's rubber; (2) To he make good the loss of 90% of the worl natural rubber resources.

HOW GOOD DRIVERS SAVE THEIR TYR AND SERVE THEIR COUNTRY

Have your tyre pressures checked every week.	Never scrape or bump the curb
Submit your tyres for replacement before the fabric is showing.	See that your brakes are even adjusted.
Never drive a commercial vehicle above its legal speed limit.	Remove stones and flints fro treads after every journey.
Avoid driving a car over 40 m.p.h.	See that your tyres are change round properly and regularly
Never corner at speed.	See that your tyres and tubes a kept in good repair.
See that wheels.— front and rear — are in proper alignment.	Avoid overloading.
Never accelerate fiercely.	Spread the load evenly.
Drive slowly over rough roads.	Avoid driving your vehicle on flat tyre.
Remember that fierce braking wastes rubber.	Take expert advice regularly the care and maintenance tyres.

HAND IN EVERY USELESS TYRE & TUB

All WORN OUT tyres and tubes—lying discarded in your garage, garden or elsewhere—are wanted at once. For they are a big and produ source of immediate rubber supply. Take yours to a local Garage for disp to a Government Depot. Or put them out with your other salvage collection by the Local Authority. Or sell them to a Merchant. SPEC COLLECTIONS of amounts over ONE TON can be obtained by wr to The Ministry of Works & Buildings, Lambeth Bridge H London, S.E.1.

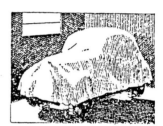

Hall's Croft, Old Town, 22nd March 1945.

Rother Street, c. 1945.

Bridge Street, c. 1945.

POET'S BIRTHPLACE

STRATFORD'S IMPORTANCE

Speaking at the annual meeting of Shakespeare's Birthplace Trustees, on Saturday, Professor J. Dover Wilson forecast an almost illimitable future for Stratford-on-Avon, because of the shrines and the theatre festivals.

He said that during his pre-war travels on the Continent, and in the Middle East, he found a great awakening of interest in the poet-dramatist, and it had been borne upon him overwhelmingly since the war began how important Stratford is.

People would be flocking to Stratford from all parts of the world in larger numbers than ever before, and the town must be ready for them.

He would like to see the museum at New Place (Shakespeare's last home) extended by the incorporation of the adjoining house, which belonged to Julian Shaw, a friend of the poet who signed his will. He suggested that Stratford Corporation might give the house to the trustees in memory of John Shakespeare, who gave them the poet and so enriched Stratford for ever.

The report showed that nearly 80,000 persons, representing 56 countries and including 23,000 from America, visited the Birthplace last year. 4.5.45

The crowds gather to see the Royal procession, 20th April 1950.

Raising money for charity with "a mile of pennies", Waterside/Bridge Foot, 1954.

High Street, c. 1955.

Indigestible!

Banter at the Naturopaths' dinner where thoughts had turned to the problem of food and the waist-line.

The Chairman (on prescribing diet): " I often have to cross out bacon."

Miss M. G. M. Phillips: " So do I—Shakespeare wrote his own plays ! "

High Street, 1955.

Henley Street, Boxing Day, 1962.

A bird's eye-view of the Memorial Theatre, looking up towards Bridge Foot, 19th April 1960.

Holy Trinity Church, mirrored in the Avon, 6th March 1964.

Bancroft Gardens, 5th October 196

Bancroft Gardens, seen from an Automobile Association spotter plane, 7th June 1967.

Bridge Street, 17th December 1966.

New Place Gardens, 10th August 1972.

Henley Street, c. 1972. The waxworks has now closed.

29th May 1972.

The swans and ducks
keep a hopeful
lunchtime vigil,
21st September 1973.

The Welcombe Hotel at Stratford-upon-Avon, only 30 minutes' drive from the National Exhibition Centre or — an unusual service, this — seven minutes by helicopter to the hotel's own landing pad, offers its visitors the perfect setting in which to relax after a bustling day at the NEC.

"We offer relaxed, friendly service in the atmosphere of a fine English country house," the hotel management says.

Executive Jet Ranger helicopters are used for transporting guests and, as these are based at Coventry airport, midway between the hotel and NEC, arrangements can be made at short notice. The cost of a flight, dependent on the numbers booked, averages £45 for one to four passengers.

The hotel's Trevelyan luncheon service is directed to executive luncheons and the cost, depending on the menu chosen, is from £20 including transfer from the NEC to hotel, luncheon and return to the NEC within two hours.

1975

PUT IT HERE

PEOPLE of Stratford and district are said to be clamouring for more space to deposit waste paper for re-cycling.

Many letters received by Mrs Muriel Pogmore stress the urgency of arranging the collection of waste materials.

She says that Mrs Abelson, Avon Croft, who started collecting paper before the election for sale for Conservative funds, has a large garage which can be used for storage. Mrs Abelson told the "Herald" anyone can deposit paper there.

Tomorrow Young Liberals plan to demonstrate at the Liberals' Ely Street headquarters how much paper is being wasted in Stratford. They collect from 300 houses and aim to show how much could be saved by council collections from the other 6,000 homes in the town. 1974

Dennis Flower and the Lord Lieutenant of Warwickshire, Mr Smith-Ryland, open Jubilee Walk (leading to Anne Hathaway's Cottage), Shottery, 1st December 1977.

Clopton Bridge clearly reveals its triple arches, which grew with road widenings. 1982.

Architects Terry Bracewell and Terry O'Neill in the entrance to the recently-opened Bridge House Medical Centre, Scholars Lane, 12th November 1982. In recent years the pair have specialised in the design of buildings for medical purposes.

The Avon snakes from left to right, with the Memorial Theatre in the centre, 22nd August 1983.

Ely Street, 30th April 1984.

View of Mary Arden's House from the Tour Bus, Wilmcote, 21st May 1986.

Bancroft Gardens, 15th April 1988.

Rother Street, 1986.

Shottery School, May 1990.

94   Penny Lane (aged 4) meets a shire horse for the first time at the Shire Horse Centre, Shipston Road, 1st April 1991.

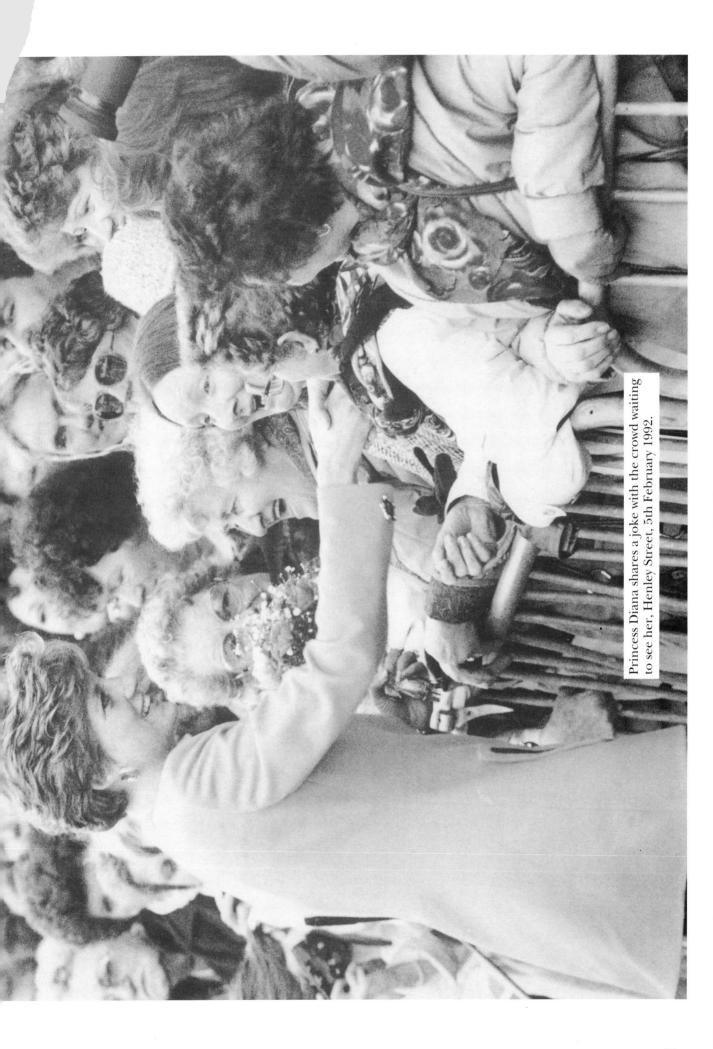

Princess Diana shares a joke with the crowd waiting to see her, Henley Street, 5th February 1992.

STRATFORD SHOP
45 Wood Street, Stratford-upon-Avon

*The easy way to book
your theatre seats,
dinner and
overnight stay*

ACKNOWLEDGEMENTS
(for providing photographs, for encouragement and numerous other favours)

Stan Ashton; Robert Bearman; Bee Cee Enterprises; Cyril and Roxanne Bennis; Big Bear Records; Birmingham Post and Mail Ltd.; Nell Blackburn; Black Swan/Dirty Duck; Jim Boulton; Richard Boyden; Dave Carpenter; Joyce Clement; David Coull; Coventry Evening Telegraph; Trevor Cox; Jane Eborall; Mona Fortescue; John Harris & Sons; Pam Harris; Val Hastings; William Hayward; Don Henderson; Betty Holte; Chris Hughes; Dave and Thelma Jones; Sheila Moore; Hedli Niklaus; Pierre Picton; Gill Pugh; Reed Midland Newspapers; Eric and Dorothy Reeves; St Gregory's R.C. Junior and Infants' School; Dorothy Savage; Margaret Schofield; Shakespeare Birthplace Trust; Dorothy Silvester; Jim Simpson; Edgar Smith; Stratford Herald; Stratford-on-Avon District Council; Stratford-upon-Avon Butterfly Farm Ltd.; Leon Tanner; The Times; Edith Usher; Joan Wanty; Warwickshire Constabulary History Society; Bob and Joan Wilkes; Rosemary Wilkes; Albert Williams; Dorothy Willingham; Ross Yates.

Please forgive any possible omissions. Every effort has been made to include all organisations and individuals involved in the book.

Back Cover:

    Top: A typical postcard.

    Bottom: High Street is closed for traffic in an early
                 pedestrianisation experiment, 7th April 1973.
                 The scheme was not adopted.

Stratford Crime Prevention Panel

Stratford Probation

Stratford Poli